This is Daniel Cook
at the Fire Station

Kids Can Press

This is Daniel Cook.
He likes to go different places,
meet interesting people and
try new things.

Mostly I like to have fun!

Today Daniel is visiting the fire station.

Here we are!

This is Sean.
Sean is a firefighter.
He's going to show
Daniel all he needs to
know about firefighting.

Firefighters have special clothes and equipment to keep them safe from heat and flames. Their boots are made of waterproof leather or rubber, and the toes are steel-plated to protect their feet.

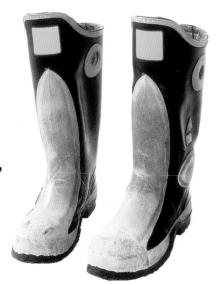

Firefighters keep their boots tucked into their pants so they can get dressed in a hurry.

What a great idea!

Firefighters' jackets and pants are made of special material that resists heat. Reflective stripes, like the kind you might wear when you ride your bike, help them be seen in the dark — and through smoke.

The boots, pants and jackets are heavy, but that's not all firefighters wear. They also need helmets, hoods, gloves and sometimes breathing masks and goggles. Together, all of that stuff weighs about 35 kg (70 lbs.).

Wow! That's almost one and a half times what I weigh. Firefighters need to be smart — and strong!

Firefighters' helmets protect their heads from heat, hits and bumps in a fire. Daniel is wearing a red captain's helmet.

What color helmets do fire captains in your neighborhood wear?

Masks help firefighters breathe clean air from special tanks they carry on their backs. The masks keep them from breathing in smoke in a fire. They might look scary, but if you see firefighters wearing masks, try not to be afraid — they're there to help you.

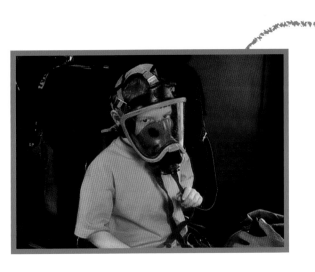

Don't be scared. It's me — really!

Clothing isn't the only thing that firefighters need to fight fires — trucks make the job much easier. Did you know that horses once pulled fire wagons? And fires were fought with bucket brigades? One person would fill a bucket with water and pass it down a line of people to be thrown at the fire.

That sounds like hard work!
I wonder if there were fire
wagons when my grandma
was little?

Now Daniel is ready to try out this fire truck.
It's red, but fire trucks can be other colors
too, like yellow, white and even green.

Daniel has a great view from the driver's seat. Sitting high above most cars and trucks, firefighters can see the traffic all around them. This also means that other drivers can see the fire truck.

Drivers need to keep both hands on the steering wheel, so the horn is a pedal you push with your foot. It's a bit far for Daniel to reach, but he gives it a good blast!

First I turn on the lights.

The switches for the lights and siren are easier to find.

Then I turn on
the siren.

The horn is
the most fun!

The fire truck has cupboards to store first aid supplies and other things the firefighters might need.

Firefighters also bring along special stuffed animals to help cheer up any kids they might see at the fire. This stuffed dog is a Dalmatian.

Dalmatians are known all over the world as firefighters' mascots. Long ago, when horses pulled fire wagons, Dalmatians helped guide the horses through the streets on the way to fires. There are no fire horses to guide today, but some fire stations keep the dogs as pets.

This fire truck also carries hoses and water. It's called a pumper truck. Hoses can be connected to different valves on the truck or to a fire hydrant to spray water on the fire.

Sometimes so much water flows through the hoses that it takes two or three firefighters to hold a single hose steady.

It's a good thing Sean as me to help him!

Fire stations near rivers, lakes and oceans have boats as part of their team of rescue vehicles. They pump water right from the lake and then shoot it out through hoses to put out fires on other boats or on buildings close to the water.

Emergency calls for the fire station come in through the dispatch room. The firefighters receive a computer printout of all the information they need to know, and an alarm sounds loudly.

There it goes now:
Wee-oooh, wee-oooh,
wee-oooh!

Then, with the lights flashing and alarm wailing, the firefighters speed off to the rescue.

That was cool!

I learned all kinds of fun things at the fire station. Now it's your turn! With your family, create an escape plan to keep you safe in case of a fire at home.

1. Together, draw a map of your house or apartment.

2. Mark where the smoke alarms are on each floor. Remind grown-ups to test the alarms every month and change the batteries once a year.

3. Draw in every window and door, and plan two ways to get out of each room in case of a fire. Buy hanging ladders for upper-story windows so you can exit safely.

4. Choose a meeting place away from your home, like a neighbor's house, a tree across the street or the mailbox on the corner. Mark your meeting place on your map.

5. At the top of the page, write down your fire department's emergency phone number and your home address. Have everyone in your family memorize them. This way you can call the firefighters for help once you are safely outside.

6. Now post your map where your family can review it regularly. Practice your escape plan using different exits. Try a fire drill with the lights out to pretend that there's smoke — if there's ever a real fire, it might be hard to see your way to the exit.

Based on the TV series *This is Daniel Cook*. Concept created by J.J. Johnson and Blair Powers. Produced by marblemedia and Sinking Ship Productions Inc.

Kids Can Press acknowledges the financial support of the Government of Ontario, through the Ontario Media Development Corporation's Ontario Book Initiative; the Ontario Arts Council; the Canada Council for the Arts; and the Government of Canada, through the BPIDP, for our publishing activity.

The producers of *This is Daniel Cook* acknowledge the support of Treehouse TV, TVOntario, other broadcast and funding partners and the talented, hard-working crew that made *This is Daniel Cook* a reality. In addition, they acknowledge the support and efforts of Deb, Murray and the Cook family, as well as Karen Boersma, Sheila Barry and Valerie Hussey at Kids Can Press.

Published in Canada by
Kids Can Press Ltd.
29 Birch Avenue
Toronto, ON M4V 1E2

Published in the U.S. by
Kids Can Press Ltd.
2250 Military Road
Tonawanda, NY 14150

www.kidscanpress.com

Written by Yvette Ghione
Edited by Karen Li
Illustrations and design by Céleste Gagnon
With special thanks to Sean Pearce of Toronto Fire Services

Printed and bound in China

The hardcover edition of this book is smyth sewn casebound.
The paperback edition of this book is limp sewn with a drawn-on cover.

CM 06 0 9 8 7 6 5 4 3 2 1
CM PA 06 0 9 8 7 6 5 4 3 2 1

Visit Daniel online at **www.thisisdanielcook.com**

Library and Archives Canada Cataloguing in Publication

Ghione, Yvette
    This is Daniel Cook at the fire station / written by Yvette Ghione.

ISBN-13: 978-1-55453-075-5 (bound)
ISBN-10: 1-55453-075-X (bound)
ISBN-13: 978-1-55453-076-2 (pbk.)
ISBN-10: 1-55453-076-8 (pbk.)

1. Fire stations—Juvenile literature. 2. Fire fighters—Juvenile literature. 3. Fire prevention—Juvenile literature. I. Title.

TH9148.G49 2006   j628.9'2   C2006-900737-3

Photo Credits

Every reasonable effort has been made to trace ownership of, and give accurate credit to, copyrighted material. Information that would enable the publisher to correct any discrepancies in future editions would be appreciated.

p. 10: Library of Congress; p. 12: (green fire truck) Susan Van Etten/Photo Edit, (yellow fire truck) Dennis MacDonald/Photo Edit; p. 17: (Dalmatians) Photo property of Bonnie Hetherington.

Kids Can Press is a ꞁ☉ꞁυƨ™ Entertainment company